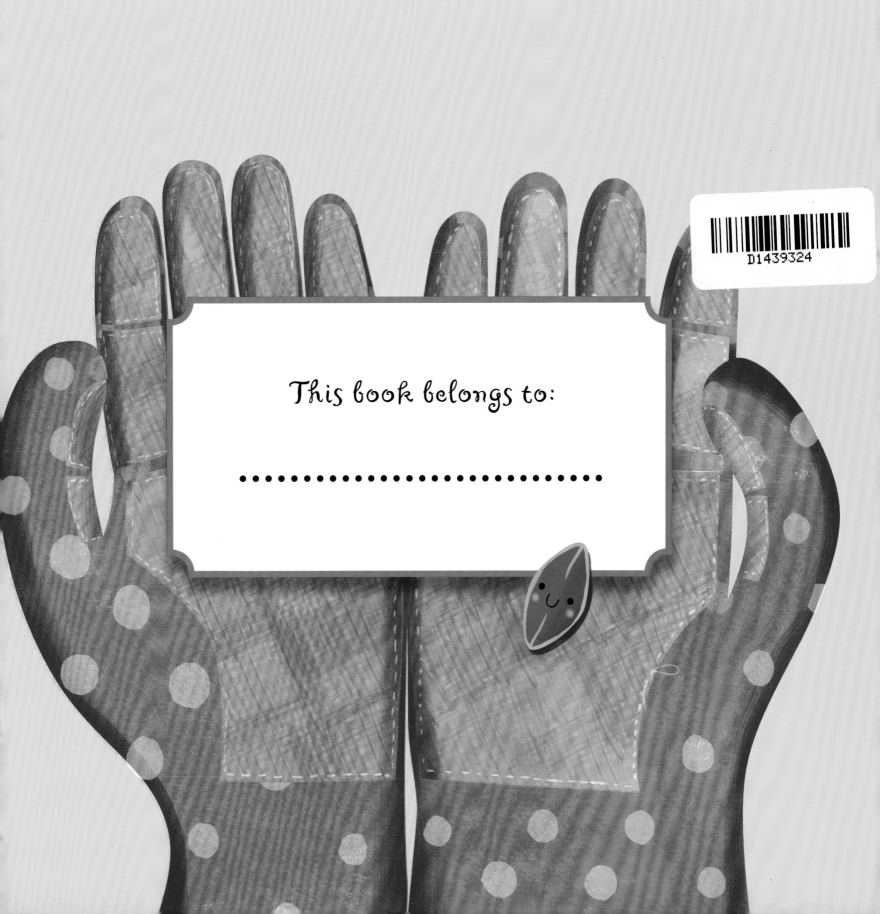

This book belongs to:

....

AUTUMN
PUBLISHING

Published in 2020
First published in the UK by Autumn Publishing
An imprint of Igloo Books Ltd
Cottage Farm, NN6 0BJ, UK
Owned by Bonnier Books
Sveavägen 56, Stockholm, Sweden
www.autumnpublishing.co.uk

1120 002
2 4 6 8 10 9 7 5 3 1
ISBN 978-1-83903-071-0

Illustrated by Gina Maldonado
Written by Suzanne Fossey

Designed by Lee Italiano
Edited by Suzanne Fossey

Printed and manufactured in China

Little
SUNFLOWER

AUTUMN
PUBLISHING

One gorgeous, springy morning, all bright and warm with sun,
the gardener came to see us. Our adventure had begun!

"I've dug a nice, fresh bed," she said, "all soft and clear of weeds. Spring's the perfect time to plant out all my lovely seeds."

She tipped me gently from the trowel into the cosy ground. The soil was soft and warm, with worms wriggling round.

She tucked me gently into bed. "There now. Off you go!"
It wasn't long before my little **shoots** began to grow.

I stretched my shoots
and – **POP!** –
I burst out of
the ground.

How **wonderful** it was
to see the garden
all around!

Day by day I
grew and **grew**.
My **big**, green
leaves unfurled.

It was nearly time to
show my petals
to the world.

I was a gorgeous sunflower, my face shining with pride.

At last,
I was all ready.
I spread my petals wide.

I heard a gentle **buzZing** and a **bee** came b**u**m**b**ling by. **"Hello, Flower,"** he said to me.

"I've brought you a surprise."

"Flowers all need pollen, so they can grow their seeds.

"We're sharing it around so every flower has what it needs."

All summer long
I chatted with the bees and butterflies.
As the weeks went by, I felt different inside.
My petals started wilting, and all round my head
I felt my tiny florets turning into seeds instead.

I started feeling sleepy. I closed my eyes and then...

... when I opened them, I found I was a seed again!

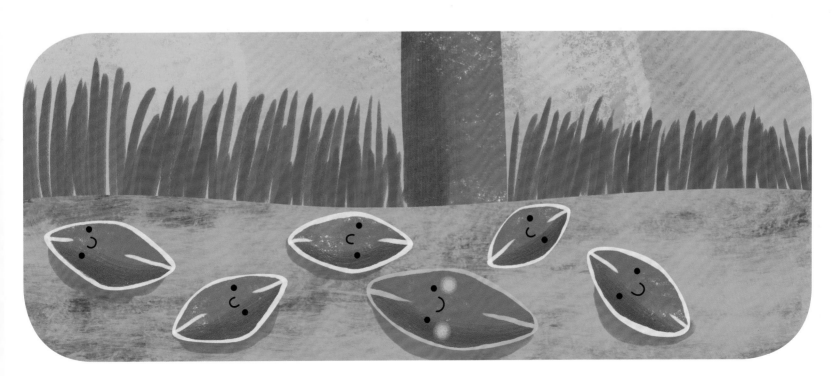

"Look at that," the gardener said.
"These seeds are just the thing.

"Let's collect them up so we can grow more flowers next spring."

They tucked us
in a packet, all
dry and safe
and warm.

"See you all next year,"
my friends said with a yawn.

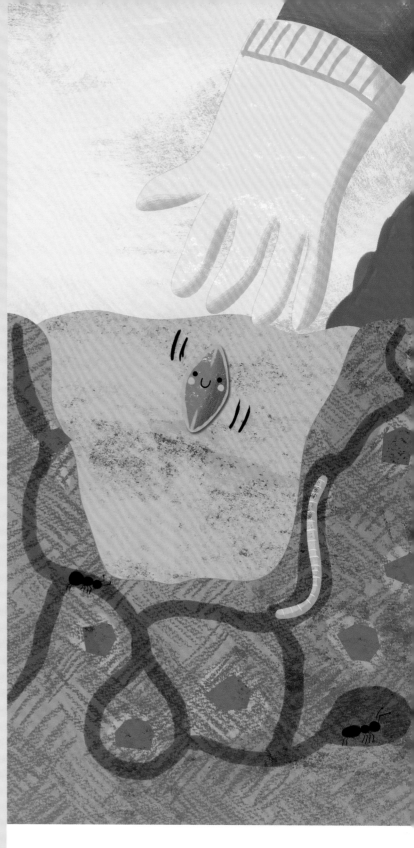

They planted me again in **spring,**   and day by day, and hour by hour,

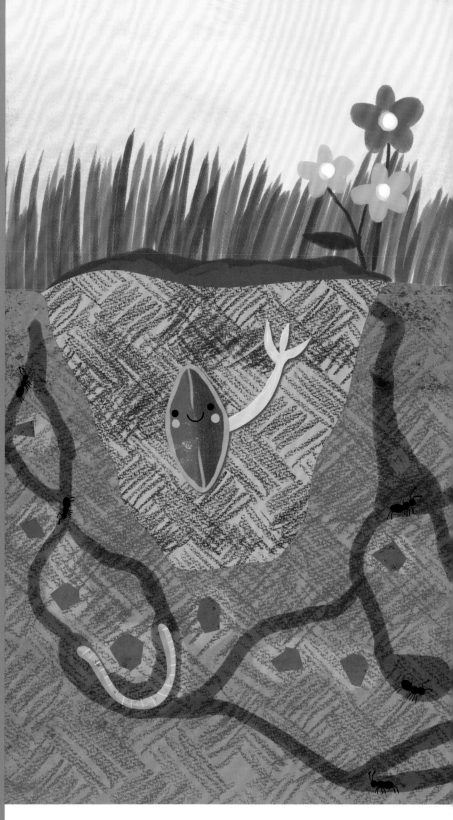

I grew and grew until I was   a beautiful...

... sunflower!

Sunflowers start as little seeds, which are planted in the ground in spring. The seed sprouts roots, which go down, and a shoot, which goes up. The shoot pushes up through the soil and starts to grow into the stem of the sunflower. During the summer, the head of the sunflower appears, with petals around the edges and hundreds of mini flowers (florets) in the middle. When insects carry pollen to the florets, they grow into seeds. At the end of the summer, the seeds in the head of the sunflower drop down onto the ground, and can be picked up and planted again next spring.